S0-CCE-737

WONDERS OF MEXICO

SOUTH OF THE BORDER

Laura Conlon

The Rourke Book Company, Inc.
Vero Beach, Florida 32964

Edited by Sandra A. Robinson

PHOTO CREDITS
© James P. Rowan: cover, pages 7, 17; © Steve Warble: title page;
© Robert Pelham: page 4; © Gary Vestal: page 8; © Francis and
Donna Caldwell: page 18; courtesy U.S. Geological Survey:
page 13 (R.E. Wilcox); courtesy Mexico's Ministry of Tourism:
pages 10 (Blake Discher), 12, 15, 21

Library of Congress Cataloging-in-Publication Data

Conlon, Laura, 1959-
    Wonders of Mexico / by Laura Conlon.
    p. cm. — (South of the border)
    ISBN 1-55916-054-3
    1. Mexico—Description and travel—Juvenile literature. I. Title.
II. Series.
F1210.C669   1994
917.204'835—dc20   94-11188
                                                              CIP

Printed in the USA

TABLE OF CONTENTS

WONDERS OF MEXICO

Mexico is a land of many wonders. Mexico has beautiful mountains, seashores and green jungles.

Ancient peoples — like the Maya, Toltec and Aztec Indians — left behind the remains of beautiful and mysterious buildings and monuments. These **ruins** tell us much about life long ago.

Mexico also has wonders made by modern people.

Ruins of Mayan buildings tower above the jungle at Uxmal on the Yucatan Peninsula

CHICHÉN ITZÁ

The Maya Indians lived in Mexico over 1,000 years ago. One of their cities was called Chichén Itzá (chee CHEN eat SAH). There the Mayans built an **observatory,** a place to study the stars and planets. They also built a pyramid nearly 1,000 feet high!

Mayans built temples to honor their gods. **Archaeologists** discovered a Mayan temple with a beautiful red stone jaguar. The jaguar was removed and put in a museum.

The Mayans built an observatory at Chichén Itzá

BUTTERFLY TREES

Among Mexico's greatest natural wonders are the "butterfly trees" in the states of Mexico and Michoacan.

Nearly 200 million monarch butterflies spend the winter in a small section of the Sierra Madre Mountains. The monarchs, like bright leaves, cover trees in the cool mountain forests.

The monarchs fly to the Sierra Madre Mountains from the United States. How they find their way is still a mystery.

Huddled together, monarch butterflies cover a tree trunk in the Sierra Madre Mountains near Mexico City

XOCHIMILCO

Xochimilco (so chee MEEL co) means "place of the field of flowers." Long ago, Xochimilcan Indians made gardens on rafts that floated on a lake. Over time, these rafts grew roots to the bottom of the lake and formed islands.

Today, tourists can ride small boats around the "floating gardens" at Lake Xochimilco.

Flat-bottomed boats glide across Lake Xochimilco

*An overlook has been built on a cliff towering above
Copper Canyon in Chihuahua, Mexico*

Mount Paracutin's lava flow nearly buried the San Juan Church in the state of Michoacan, Mexico

MOUNTAINS

Mexico's highest mountain is Mount Orizaba. At 18,700 feet, it is the third tallest peak in North America. Mount Orizaba is a very old, **extinct** volcano. Many of Mexico's mountains are volcanoes.

One of Mexico's newest volcanoes is Mount Paracutin. In 1943, farmers in Paracutin watched as ash and **lava** began to **erupt** from their cornfields through cracks in the earth. The ash and lava covered their village and created a peak 1,000 feet high.

Popocatepetl Volcano stands high above a church in the village of Cholula in the Mexican state of Puebla

COASTLINES

Mexico has more than 6,000 miles of seacoast. Miles of sandy beaches, plenty of sun and year-round warm temperatures attract many visitors to Mexico's **resort** cities. Acapulco is a famous resort city on the Pacific Coast. Cancun and Cozumel are island resorts off the Gulf Coast.

The coastal areas provide much wealth for the country. Rich deposits of oil lie undersea off Mexico's Gulf Coast. Off both coasts, fish are plentiful.

A sliver of white sand separates rocky cliffs and the Caribbean Sea at Tulum National Park

CATHEDRALS

Many of Mexico's large Roman Catholic churches, or cathedrals, are wonders of art and design.

Roman Catholics from around the world visit one of these churches — the Cathedral of the Virgin of Guadalupe. It was built on the land where Juan Diego said he was visited in 1531 by the Virgin Mary, mother of Jesus.

Many of Mexico's large Roman Catholic churches are wonders of art and design

MURALS

Ancient Indians painted huge pictures on the walls of temples and palaces. These **murals** told stories of their lives and their gods.

In modern Mexico, many buildings are decorated with murals showing Mexico's history. One of the most famous murals is on the library at the University of Mexico. The beautiful design was made with over 7 million tiny stones.

A mural in Mexico City shows ancient warriors

PLAZA DE TOROS MONUMENTAL

The largest bullfighting ring in the world is the Plaza de Toros Monumental in Mexico City. Nearly every Sunday, people come to watch the sport that was brought to Mexico by Spanish explorers.

The crowd cheers as the **matador,** or bullfighter, uses his bright red cape to lead the bull around in circles. The fight ends when the matador stabs the tired bull with a sword.

Glossary

ancient (AIN chent) — very old

archaeologist (are kee AHL a jist) — a scientist who studies artifacts and other remains of ancient cultures

erupt (eh RUPT) — to burst out

extinct (ex TINKT) — no longer active

lava (LAH vuh) — melted rock that erupts from a volcano and later hardens

matador (MAT uh door) — a bullfighter

mural (MYUR uhl) — a decorative painting made directly on a wall

observatory (ob ZERV a tor ree) — a building with special scientific equipment for looking at the stars

resort (re ZORT) — a place where people often go for a vacation

ruins (ROO inz) — the remains of an ancient building or city

INDEX